· THE JOY OF AVERY SERIES ·

SAY YES AGAIN

RHONDA WAGNER
ILLUSTRATED BY KIMBERLY GROVES

LUCIDBOOKS

Say YES Again

Copyright © 2022 by Rhonda Wagner
Illustrated by Kimberly Groves

Published by Lucid Books in Houston, TX
www.LucidBooksPublishing.com

All rights reserved. No part of this publication may be reproduced, stored in a retrieval system, or transmitted in any form by any means, electronic, mechanical, photocopy, recording, or otherwise, without the prior permission of the publisher, except as provided for by USA copyright law.

Scripture taken from the Holy Bible: International Standard Version®. Copyright © 1996-forever by The ISV Foundation. ALL RIGHTS RESERVED INTERNATIONALLY. Used by permission.

ISBN: 978-1-63296-510-3 (Hardback)
ISBN: 978-1-63296-509-7 (Paperback)
eISBN: 978-1-63296-508-0

Special Sales: Most Lucid Books titles are available in special quantity discounts. Custom imprinting or excerpting can also be done to fit special needs. Contact Lucid Books at Info@LucidBooksPublishing.com.

To
Avery,
my loquacious granddaughter, who brings so much joy.

And, to her parents,
Lisa and JJ,
who obeyed God's call to become foster parents.

And especially,
to
our Heavenly Father,
who can be trusted to write the most beautiful stories for our lives,
"more than all we can ask or imagine" (Ephesians 3:20)!

Dedicated to the many foster families
who continue to
say **YES** again!

Read more of this family's story of foster care and their
mission to provide hope and encouragement at
www.messintoamessage.com,
or follow on Instagram @lisa_messintoamessage.

Mom and Dad were bringing a new placement home today.
Avery was glad her parents said YES to the call.
"David is only two days old, Nana!" Avery said.

Nana smiled.
"Yes! A new baby is something to celebrate!"
So they had baked a cake.

Pop was outside blowing up balloons.
Sometimes he used too much air!

Pop!

Avery dashed out the door to help her grandfather.

"Watch me leap like a frog, Pop!" Avery squealed.
She squatted low and jumped high off the porch.

"How about you leap over here, dear?" Pop suggested.

Up, up, and away!
Avery soared over to help.

"Can you hold the balloons while I tie these strings?" Pop asked.

"Yes, I can, Pop!"

They finished decorating the light post as Mom and Dad pulled in.

Avery ran to see the baby.
"He's asleep, Dad!" she whined.

Dad shrugged.
"I guess big roads make David sleepy, just like you."

Inside, Mom placed the baby into Avery's arms.

She cuddled him close and whispered,
"I'm your sister, David. And you're my brother."

She didn't want to call him a foster brother. Avery loved the baby already and never wanted to say goodbye. She looked at the picture on the wall of her first foster brother. She missed Zander and wondered if he missed her too.

After everyone ate a slice of yummy cake, Nana and Pop left for home.

"Will you grab me a diaper, Avery?" Dad asked while feeding David.

"Yes, I will!" Avery said as she twirled over to the box. She balanced a diaper on her head while carefully walking an imaginary tightrope back.

"Ta-da!" Avery bowed.

The diaper fell from her head right onto Dad's lap.

"Thanks!" Dad chuckled.

Avery grinned and bowed again.

She watched Dad change David's diaper and put him to bed. She watched Mom make bottles for night feedings.

Then Dad announced, "Bedtime for all **Big Sisters!** Tomorrow is another day."

In the morning, Avery peeked at David in his crib.

"He sleeps a lot, Mom!" Avery said.

"Yes," Mom agreed, "but he will wake up hungry soon."

"He eats a lot too!" Avery said.

"Every two to four hours," Mom yawned while pouring more coffee.

Avery liked being a Big Sister in a foster family, but David wasn't much of a playmate.

On Fridays, an agency worker picked David up for his birth family visits.
One morning while he was away, Mom's phone rang.
"YES!" Mom said. "We can provide respite care this weekend."

"Luca is 10 years old. Just a couple years older than you,"
Mom told Avery after the call.
"He needs a safe place to stay until his new foster family gets home from a trip. His brother lives with them already."

Avery had never been a **Younger Sister** before.
She felt excited to have an older playmate.

"Do you want to pick out a backpack for Luca?" Mom asked.
"Yes, I do!" Avery replied.
She chose an orange backpack from the closet where they kept extras.

That afternoon Luca arrived with his caseworker.
Mom and Luca's worker talked while Avery showed off her brother.

"Meet David," Avery said. "Asleep again."

"Wow! He's so little," Luca replied. "Did you know I have a brother?"

"Yes. Mom told me." Avery said.

"And we're finally going to live together!" he said.

Avery wondered why they had been separated.
She felt sure if Mom and Dad got a call for two siblings,
they would say YES and YES again.

"Let's all go outside and play," said Mom.
Avery and Luca played catch with Dad while Mom pushed David in the stroller.

Soon their neighbor dropped by in that old, beat-up truck.

Clickety-Clack! **Bang!**

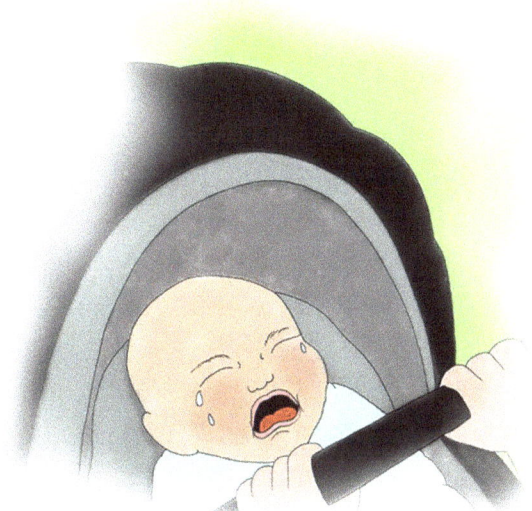

The baby cried and Luca ran.

"Wait for me, Luca!" Avery yelled.
"Where are you? Are we playing hide and seek?"

Avery looked for Luca behind the big oak tree.

Mom looked between the shrubs.

The neighbor looked under the porch.

Dad looked beside the barn.

Dad found Luca,
shaking in his shoes.
He sat down beside him.

"Let's go in the house, Avery."
Mom said.

"They'll be in later."

Avery was confused, "I didn't know Luca wanted to hide."

"I don't think he wanted to hide," Mom said. "The noise from that old truck probably reminded Luca of something scary."

"Like thunder?" Avery wondered.

"I don't know," Mom said. "We haven't walked in his shoes."

"Walked in his shoes?" Avery asked.

"It means to put yourself in his place, to think about what his life is like."

Avery thought of Luca beside the barn talking with Dad.

"Luca is safe here, Mom." Avery said.

"He is," Mom agreed. "But he needs to *feel* safe."

At bedtime, Avery prayed,

"Dear God, please help Luca *feel* safe while he's here.
Show me how I can help.
Amen."

She crawled into bed and fell asleep.

Avery dreamed about . . .
SHOES!
Big shoes!
Little shoes!

Shoes like Luca's!
Shoes like David's!
She even tried walking in their shoes!

The next morning, Avery told Luca about the dream in her most loquacious way! She loved to talk!

"Yours, of course, were **too big!**" she exclaimed. "Then I tried to squeeze my feet into itty bitty shoes like David wears! **Yowza! Super ouchy!**"

Luca laughed until his sides hurt.

Later that day, Avery told Dad about her dream.

"I was *trying* to walk in their shoes, Dad," Avery laughed.

Dad chuckled. "Well, it's good to think about living in another's shoes. If their life is hard in ways that ours isn't, we can offer to help."

"That's why we say YES to foster care, right?" Avery asked.

"Yes, indeed!" Dad replied.

Avery and Luca were the best of friends for three days.
They rode bikes.
They skipped rocks in the pond.
They even caught a few frogs and named them all.

And then – Luca was leaving.

"I'm gonna be with my brother!" Luca smiled and waved goodbye.

"Show him how to skip rocks!" Avery shouted.

Avery would miss Luca, but she was glad he would be with his brother. It was a very-happy-and-just-a-little-bit-sad-at-the-same-time day.

David was awake more often now.
He smiled and cooed when Avery wiggled his toes.

"Tickle!
Tickle!"

Avery loved watching David grow,
but after three months,
he was leaving too.

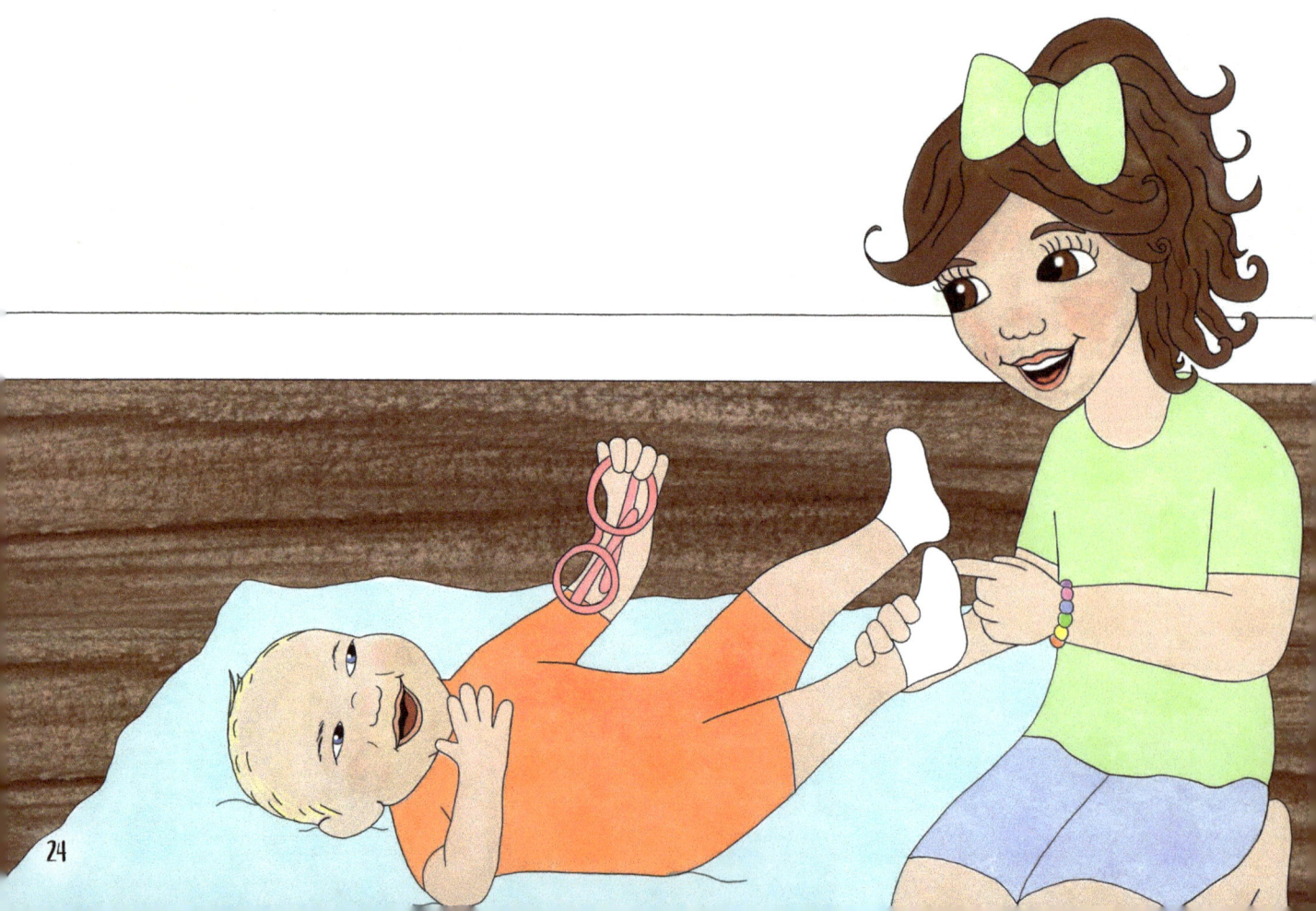

"If he's not going home to his parents, why can't he stay here?" Avery cried. "We love him!"

"We do," Mom sniffed.

"But his aunt and uncle love him too."

"It's called a kinship placement," Dad explained. "Kin means family. Usually, it's best if children can stay with biological family."

Avery sighed. "I know family should be together."

And then – David was gone.

Avery cuddled her cats while Dad and Mom hung pictures of Luca and David near Zander's picture.

"Do they look straight, Avery?" Mom asked.

"They look fine," Avery said with a pout.

Mom sat down beside her.

"Let's imagine what they're doing!" Mom said.

"I imagine Zander coming down the slide with his biggest smile and his parents waiting to catch him.

Your turn."

Avery smiled. "I imagine Luca showing his brother how to skip rocks! He was getting really good at it!

Your turn, Dad."

"Hmmm. David? He's probably asleep again!" They all laughed.

Avery loved her family. She was glad they said YES to foster care. Avery beamed at her parents and asked,

"When can we say YES again?"

Dear Reader,

I hope you like my story so far and will tell your friends about it because more people need to know about foster care! More moms and dads should go to school to become foster parents like mine. There are so many children who need a place to live where families will give their best love. And the rules really aren't so bad.

Be brave as a family, and contact a local agency soon! You are in this together. Once you say yes to the call of foster care, you will want to say yes again! And remember, you don't have to worry about it. But it's okay to wonder.

With love and joy,
Avery

Glossary

Agency worker/Caseworker — someone licensed to work alongside a child in foster care and their biological family to aid in the reunification process or secure permanency for the child

Biological — related by birth, not through marriage, foster care, or adoption

Birth family — the family a child is born into

Foster brother — a boy being raised by your parents while in foster care

Foster family — a family who is licensed to care for children in the foster care system

Kinship placement — when a child in foster care is placed with a relative, family friend, or person in close relation to their birth family

Loquacious — talkative, chatty (someone like Avery)

Placement — a child who has been removed from their home and is assigned temporary safe housing with a foster family

Respite care — one family temporarily cares for another family's foster child(ren) in order to provide relief and/or assistance

Siblings — children who have at least one shared birth parent or are adopted or fostered by your parents

Conversation Starters
New Placement (pages 1–4)

While it's always exciting to meet a new placement, it's not always appropriate to celebrate their arrival. Babies are exciting, and as Nana says, "A new baby is something to celebrate." But the emotional trauma of an older child experiencing removal would not permit such a celebration, although a new toy or other welcoming gifts may be comforting for a child of any age.

- Would you like to pick out a new toy for our foster child?

Roles of Extended Family Members (pages 1-3)

Openly discuss the involvement of extended family—expectations, preparations, background checks for childcare, and more. When extended family members jump on board to love foster children unconditionally, it helps a foster family thrive.

- Are you excited for your grandparents, aunts, uncles, and cousins to meet your foster sibling?

Your Biological* Child's Feelings and Questions (pages 5, 11, 16, 25)

It is important to encourage open discussion with biological children about new feelings that are hard to understand. Family dynamics are changed, routines are disrupted, and departures are hard.

If this is not your first placement, your biological children will bring feelings and questions based on previous experiences and end results. In this story, as early as the first day of a new placement, Avery is thinking about the hard goodbye and doesn't want to do it. She remembers how much it hurt.

Parents need to speak often of reunification as the primary end goal. Reminders of "while he is here," "hoping he can go home," and "helping for a while" will help prepare your child for a goodbye in the future. Of course, this language would change if reunification was no longer an option.

- Does it make you glad to know we are helping him for a while?
- Would you like to pray that his family is able to get back together again?

Birth Order (pages 6, 8, 9)

Foster families have the option to preserve the birth order of their biological children or to mix the birth order up as foster children come and go in their family. It's an important conversation to have as you become licensed and think through what would be the best dynamic for your family.

In our story, Avery had never been a Younger Sister because her parents chose to maintain birth order with Avery as the oldest child. In the case of short-term respite care, they allowed an exception.

- What do you think about an older child staying with us for a while?

Birth Family Visits (page 9)

Typically, foster children visit with their birth parents weekly and sometimes multiple times per week. Talk through how this could impact your family's routines.

- What do you think a birth family visit might be like for your foster sibling?
- We might drive the child to the agency for a visit. Would you like to ride along to do that? Or the child might get picked up at our home by an agency worker.

Respite Stay (pages 9-11)

Share with your biological children what you know about a child coming for a short-term respite stay. Explain how to make another child feel "at home" and "invited" during their time with your family. A small gift is welcoming but not necessary. Friendly games rather than competitive games are best.

- Do you think we should play catch in the yard to help him feel comfortable with us?
- What are some other ideas you have for fun while he's here?

Sibling Separations (page 11)

Keeping siblings together should be a priority as a foster family. Children who have been removed from all they know benefit greatly from the connectedness of siblings. Sometimes this cannot happen because a foster family's home may be full when a foster child's sibling is in need of placement, or a family who has adopted through care may no longer be licensed when a sibling needs a home. But healthy sibling relationships should be pursued whenever possible and safe.

- Do you think Luca and his brother should live together?
- If we get a call for siblings, do you think we should say yes to more than one child?
- You might have to share your room if we do that. Is that okay with you?

Trauma & Triggers (pages 13-16)

Every foster child has endured trauma. Whether from neglect or abuse, there is a reason removal has taken place. Removal itself is traumatic for a child. Triggers should be expected. Talk age appropriately with your biological child about situations a foster child might have endured.

- Were you surprised when Luca ran and hid when the truck made a loud noise?
- What kinds of noises make you feel scared?

Safe vs. Feeling Safe (pages 17-18)

You know your home offers a safe environment. But there is a big difference between a child being safe and feeling safe in your home. When a surprisingly emotional response occurs with a child in your care, it may be due to a trauma trigger. Your biological child may wonder why a parent's response is different from the response typically given to them if they act out. Remind your child of their safe home and your love for them.

Discuss age appropriately with your biological child why a foster child might seem to overreact. Talk about "putting on another's shoes" and imagining what their life might have been like before they arrived.

- Do you think Luca was safe at Avery's house? If so, why didn't he feel safe?
- Are there times you don't feel safe?

Kinship Placement (page 25)

While a child is in care, agency workers continue to actively search for safe and suitable extended family members. If caseworkers find appropriate extended family members, children are often moved to that home. Kinship placements can often provide more frequent visitation for the child and biological parents and allow biological family relationships to be preserved.

- Did you understand why David was leaving Avery's family to live with his aunt and uncle?

The Hard Goodbye (pages 23-25)

Does it ever get any easier? These kids take a piece of your heart when they go, and you fear the piece they will take from your child's heart. Your biological child has loved and lost a sibling. It hurts. Yet they learn as we parents do too that helping and loving that child when they needed it most is so worth it. Parents and their children alike may want to say yes again right away, while others may need a break after a hard goodbye. It's important to have this conversation after each hard goodbye as breaks can be healthy and healing too.

- Are you glad we are a foster family?
- Do you want to say YES again like Avery does?

*Biological is used as an all-inclusive word for children who are permanently within a family's home, including biological, adopted, and those under legal guardianship.

Avery is a young girl who loves mysteries and surprises and her little family who lives on a little road. This very talkative child has been a Big Sister in a foster family six times (not counting short-term respite stays when she's also been a Younger Sister) and has experienced three different placement outcomes:

reunification, kinship placement, and adoption.

Stay tuned for Book 4 of *The Joy of Avery* series when Avery does not experience a hard goodbye but the joy of adoption instead.

It's Okay to Wonder
Book 1

Helps children understand their feelings as the family prepares their home and their hearts for foster care.

Braver Than Me
Book 2

Helps children understand their feelings when a foster child arrives, becomes part of the family, and says a hard goodbye.

Say YES Again
Book 3

Helps children understand their feelings as hard goodbyes continue and compassion for the child in care grows.

Stay connected at
www.TheJoyOfAverySeries.com

Acknowledgments

Thank you,
Lisa Robertson,
for your valuable input as a foster parent and your love as a daughter.

Thank you,
Sara Triana Mitchell,
for making me stretch for something better with your skillful edits.

Thank you,
Kimberly Groves,
for your imaginative and playful illustrations that bring this book to life.

Thank you,
Jamie Sandefer,
for your gift of friendship and guidance to connect with Lucid Books.

And thank you to my husband,
Dan,
for continuing to encourage me in this endeavor.

May all glory be to God in these combined efforts.

About the Author and Illustrator

Rhonda Wagner is a writer who lives with her husband in western Pennsylvania where she was born. They have two married daughters and four grandchildren who live in northeastern Ohio. She was inspired to write *The Joy of Avery* series when her younger daughter and son-in-law became foster parents. As a foster grandma, she is passionate about giving her very best love to all her grandchildren, foster and forever.

Find her online at www.rhondawagnerbook.com.

Kimberly Groves grew up in the beautiful mountains of West Virginia. Kim and her husband Justin enjoy raising their daughters on those same mountaintops. Art has always been a huge part of Kim's life, and she continues to follow that passion by bringing images to life with the stroke of a pencil or paintbrush.

www.ingramcontent.com/pod-product-compliance
Lightning Source LLC
LaVergne TN
LVHW070948070426
835507LV00028B/3454